To the God
of Rain

for Miranda,
for Joe

To the God
of Rain
TIM LIARDET

seren

Seren is the book imprint of
Poetry Wales Press Ltd
Nolton Street, Bridgend, Wales
www.seren-books.com

ISBN 1-85411-335-6

A CIP record for this title is available from the British Library

The publisher acknowledges the financial assistance
of the Arts Council of Wales

Printed in Palatino by Bell & Bain, Glasgow

Cover: *Those Who Stay* (detail), left panel of *States of Mind* tryptich,
        Umberto Boccioni, 1911
        Digital Image © 2003 The Museum of Modern Art / Scala,
        Florence
        Photo © Scala, Florence

Contents

I want to explore the sufferings of an electric light-bulb
Umberto Boccioni, *Dinamismo plastico*, 1914

In the midst of the confusion of departure the mingled
abstract sensations are translated into force-lines and
rhythms in quasi musical harmony ... the excitement
of 'Those Who Go' is expressed in dynamic horizontal
green lines which contrast with the pale perpendiculars
of 'Those Who Stay'.
Umberto Boccioni, *La Voce*, 1911

The sixteen people you have around you in a tram in
rapid motion are one, ten, four, three; they stand in place
and at the same time are in movement; they go and come,
are projected out into the street and swallowed up by a
patch of sunlight, then suddenly are back in their seats.
Umberto Boccioni, *Manifesto dei pittori futuristi*, 1910

To Dvořák's Cello Concerto in B Minor

And the whole thrown, threshing chaos of it
can seem to act out to a soundtrack
as if responding to lip-sync or choreography
or the reception of good news, so every part
seems to sing to every other part which seems
to sing back, everything sings to everything:
caught in the spell of the cellist you
forgive the world its many wheezy indiscretions
and learn to notice the dog-daisies rocking
their raft of light through the window, also in the spell:
they remind me of the latest segment of crowd
swept up in the wave, responding then relaxing.
No they don't. They remind me more
of the latest note on the cello about
to sprout a yellow heart and be born
in a shatter of petals, joining the rich swathes
of haulms that brush the summer dust at will
backwards and forwards across the glass.

Needle on Zero

The unexpected power cut left the clocks
in every room regurgitating nought after nought –
you are leaving. The train approaches. Things start to shake.
The number of days and of nights
and the number of hours and of minutes, rattle over at speed
like the destinations on the departure board.
Look. The old world snaps like a wishbone.
As easy as that, with hardly a protest.
It was the words you spoke, so few, which left
the marital home as rubble and a fine dust to descend
like snow onto your shoes, wiped to a half moon.
And you step out from it – while every fin
of your watch's tiny universe begins to spin –
in new coat, high heels, your brilliant skin.

A Futurist Looks at a Dog

I do not see godmother's adoring pet
as you do, nor know him by name; neither can
I keep the present he keeps:
his six little steps to match godmother's one.

I see instead every stride the dog has made
in the last twenty metres at once,
the sum of strides per second jumbled up
on top of one another: its tail

a cactus of wags, its rapid legs
a sort of tailback of centipedes,
a strobile of stunted steps, a carwash brush,
two bleary propellers rotating.

Above it, the leash in flight is many leashes
whipping and overlapping,
a flung silver net, a soundwave,
each stride a new species of leash;

the dachshund once set in motion
embarks upon another existence,
and godmother's pet as you know him
vanished twenty, no, thirty strides back.

11

Laws of Probability

So your feisty stepmother and my therapist,
one October, though we did not know it, got to mount
the same ornate elephant in the extreme North

of Uttar Pradesh – seven thousand miles from home –
with as much exquisite apathy as if they shared
the Tube from Baker Street to Euston Square.

They shrieked, we may presume, and held onto their hats
that far east of the great Syrian desert,
and did not for a seasick moment suspect how close

to you and I they came, sat back to back,
– quanta of heat trembling in the spaces.
To me it seems as likely they should meet

as the two of them should conspire to find
the one mosquito in Goa with a ring on its back leg.
So picture them, their shoulder-blades touching,

oblivious for a while to their respective flocks
of deferred or inherited children,
flung out on the long stopping curve and jostling up

between the loose petals of their blouses
a pocket of warm and inconsequential air,
a new species of commonplace.

Exile

Your expatriate father says he is *going native*.
So that's what being caught
in flagrante delicto with the maid Orila is.
His suitcases and rackets are once again
stood in the hall. There are fewer and fewer.

Out there in the light of superlative exile
and of the pale Indian Ocean
he is leaving again, leaving what cannot be fixed,
rejecting forgiveness in favour
of making farewells. There are more and more.

He has passed down the restive gene
to all three of his daughters
like a moth in a jar, making that feathery noise.
And heads out further and further east
scratching lines in dirt, treasuring but a stick
or two of ethnic furniture.

Or perhaps he is swung out precariously
like the old grand over the narrow street,
too far out by now to go back,
too close to its dents in the rug to be eased down

it gongs from wall to wall, just hangs there, eluding both
grandma's slipping grip and the sterling-smelling shark.

A Haunting of X Lovers

Dead haloes, whiffs, the scars of mattress-buttons,
a language shared for a while now banished
to the lexicon of loss,
mere vapour, she says, mere vapour:

the heat we make causes the vapour to rise
– a Chinese wrestle of perfumes.
Are they here? No, no. Simply the gnat-storm
of their pheromones – the threat they may return.

Simply the neat, babylike bruises caused
by their grip along the whole length of his spine
like something bumming a ride,
bending it like an umbrella rib, or cello string;

yes, their hands, so tiny, as if compressed by light
once the body has disappeared,
dropped away from where it hung;
confusion as to who let go of whom. Or did not.

Shoo! She claps, and like a bush full of Cabbage-whites
they show themselves as if his spine
comes briefly into flower, comes briefly into leaf
before it is merely a spine again.

Paris

1

They went to chilly Paris in March and he had to borrow her eyes
because his reading spectacles were still with the optometrist:
sixty to pay for the lenses, sixty more for the frames.
So it was the map of the old symmetrical city seemed
a fabulous blur, like the pipe-dream of the squinting pointillist
or hunger of the lens for the vision it cannot decipher
though it knows it is out there, blotched and flying.
And was this not, he thought, was this not a further skirmish
with the furtive agent of the lensmaker's art?
Read me, he said to her, give me Paris in the names of its captains
and cardinals, generals, psychologists and saints.
Station upon station, street by street, supply the voice
able to spell out but not pronounce the names
of a language you do not speak, guide me through the tag-lines,
the spiel for the next exhibit, the bottom half underwater:
so waist-deep in language, he thought being unable
to trace on the page the city's landmarks meant missing
the real thing in three dimensions, oddly vertical.
If you'll be my lenses, he said, perch them on my nose
while our round welts pin on the pavement one beastlike shadow
and our hands are in the pockets of each other's coat.
Bring me Paris magnified, as if picking out the gleam
upon the toecap of the Egyptian waiter's shoe in the crowded café;
you deal with the trees, while I tackle the bleary forest.

2

Lead me, he said, to the most exhausted visage in Paris,
pick out a critical path through the pickpockets,
walk me down level after windy level of the steps.
So he had his nearsighted woman read him from place to place:
words pressed on him, tipsy metaphors, remote
as the names of constellations. *Concorde, Pigalle, Jules Joffrin.*
Too long inspecting them like the hairs on his arm
had left his eyes a little bleary, if not migrainous:
so even if he met Paris he might mistake it for something else,
an omphalos of scraps, say, an outbreak of fire-escapes
coming down vertical out of an onrushing sky,
a carapace of cobbles, an orchestra of horns.
It assembles for us to arrive in, he said, crossed
by the latest cloud-edge, then sun. Its monuments dim
then brighten, he said, as he tripped on a curb of words.
So feel for its braille of stones, its bumps and lumps,
the great spirit is escaping everywhere and the rest is footslog.
The city wraps us round, airy and curvaceous,
as if every flying vision tickles my optic nerve
and the gargoyles look down, as I look up. So *read* –
teach us, like venerable Chang and Eng, how to live with this
cross-Channel, weird dependence, sharing sleeves and eyes;
shed by twenty/twenty vision like a hole by its glove, he said,
mislaid by my spectacles, I stroke your cuff.

3
Like the lovebirds on the Quai De La Megisserie
swivel round, they said, explore the neighbourhood,
look up, look down, ruffle up or peep, but come back always
to earth a thousand foreign strangenesses at 0 degrees.
Because my spectacles are locked in the optometrist's drawer,
he said, language shrinks. Vowels drift by, looking
for something to couple with. Adjectives queue for the Louvre.
Give me Paris, he said again, and give it to me first
a sticky bud, a boulevard at a time. When I breathe
rags of steam into the prism-ring and throw arms in the air,
you click, X marks the spot. But what of the rest
of Paris behind us, like the mind, enduring the power cut
that keeps the shore's million pebbles as undiscovered
as the sapphires cluttering up the Rue Saint Honoré,
lost to us, because we alight here, in the ring?
Collar up, in hound's tooth, read on but keep us
from overload, while I squinny. If we cannot gather
so much distinguished rubble in our arms let us
settle for our fragments, spilt all along the way between
the Rembrandt exhibition and the bottom step to the Metro.
If the place is as hard to leave as to reach you must
help me to read, he said, the labels on our suitcases
should they elude me like old friends. Our bags will otherwise
go round and round forever, stuck in the groove.

Café Ruc

after Brassaï

After the bumper-to-bumper chaos and glitz
of the jewellery quarter, as if stunned, we fall into
this equally crowded café, squeezed up next
to a less smitten couple, also held in the mirrors
that quadruple the place's dimensions and get us
from four different angles at once,
as if we surround ourselves, alert in every strand:
right profile, back, you talking, the view of us from above.

I am in Paris with you. It provides us with this evidence.
It offers us these four visions of our vanishing point
in one grasp, spins us from its crowds
into total awareness, responding in every hair;
where there is suddenly less space,
suddenly four times as much, at our elbows.
Were you wearing a soft and floppy hat, say mignonette,
I'd stroke its brim, and lift it up.

So it is we arrive at the source
of quadruple meaning, deep inland. Even the air is plural.
We are ourselves, we are strangers in the corner,
reflections of each other. We are objects of light.
There is light here, and glass,
light and glass and the reflection of light and glass.
When the four cloned and stooping waiters arrive our wave
breaks all around us softly, streets away.

Distiller's Unstable Daughter Explains her Absence from the Class

The men have come out of the ground again.
I have to tell you the successful distiller
of spirits has a seventh tall daughter.

Listen. They call me from under the street.
They lean on shovels, down under the awning
in the hole in the pavement, exposing the bright wires.

They wear hard-hats, and though not magicians
will restore to me my visibility:
green eye, breast, gangling leg, painted toe-nail.

Yes, they ease me back into view. And I, slipping
in and out of my most perfect of minds –
monster of my yellow psychiatrist – step down

into the sunlight. The sex is clean and necessary.
The orange awning, warmed from the inside, contains
the closest approximation of day.

Now that I can be seen, I am lethal. See –
my *vividness*. But will my six sisters and mother
and distillery-owning father deep into their storm

have the eyes, the twenty / twenty vision
against the old glaucoma, the eclipsed pupil?
Now there is a question for the red optometrist.

Tremble

There are those who leave. And you are leaving.
The train approaches us and things begin to shake:
the string set singing in the upright grand sets off
the filament in the bulb, and passes on
a tremor through the drawer of misted spoons,
disturbing on the squeaky half moons of the hooks
a jostle of cups soft as cow-bells. Disturbed
by the thunder of the overwhelming question
you are changing shape, like liquid gas – Brynhyld, say,
into Molly Bloom, clockwork mouse into lioness, and just
in case you doubt your stomach for it, see how
what you thought was a shadow turns into a heron
hunched in the wings of your hair which flops to break
over the beam of your bicycle lamp, like a cloak.

Tremble, Tremble

It is *you* I address, longstriding girl, you who are
incomparably you, boundary-scorning although
you walk with folded arms, as prone to outrage
as to injury, as slyly, obliquely courageous as
you are cautious to move and yet can make things shake,
things shake, things shake; but also those
in the evening Underground crowd into which a drop of you
distils like the fine octanes in its blood,
a single drip, getting the heartbeat to pound
against the sternum, to throb in the navel.
It is you I address, and them, or the bit
of you that lives, or abides, or resonates
in those of them who ever knew the sea-change
into something rich and strange.

The Aviary

I have dreamed it again – the glass aviary which
I half knew all along was up there in the stuffy attic.
Birds! Ex-reptiles. Plovers in the house! They let out
a zoological racket, or else the roof felt muffles it.
The rips in the felt so shredded by spilling light,
it is hard to pick one species from the rest.
At heights from which they squirt yoghurt to lambast
order, and rain feathers, spinning out mid-air
their arse-up burlesque of a tuning orchestra
I find hundreds of birds trying out their noise indoors:
they have everything to do with the furniture's
shrouds, splashed like painters' overalls. There are shrikes
in the rafters wittering, like provincial hacks;
tits that send the sound of a squeaking laundry basket wheel
into the long pipes, echoing. And all
of them must spiel and gossip separately until
consensus calls them together, and Verona green
smudges to scarlet, to olive and yellow, to wine.
And though my hands feel in the way a braille of glass
that on closer inspection encases the space,
its sense of inner light and liberty seems to be
the incubator of a million watt joy,
pitched between its floor of eggshells and the height
only the highest notes can reach. But what
of the as-yet-feeble, almost sickly kitten struggling out
of its shell inside the brilliant glass and yet
to stretch in its ragged furs and stand on its feet?

The Wasps' Nest

"The hole through which everything poured, beneath
    the rug..."
wrote Liu Hsün, but we had a wasps' nest.
Almost as if our great room of desk and clock
    and wing-chair had begun to sag

and sink, where some keep cash, we had a wasps'
    nest. And board after board
blocked the view. So did the rug.
Beneath castors and claw-feet – though its
    towers and ladders were crude –

it began to draw at the whole house, bowed the long
    joist beneath us
like the weight of the afterlife.
It toiled in its place like an engine softly burning gas

on the wick of itself, dipped deep. And this was
    strange. We feared
the flame of it. Not that
it seemed to threaten us but the heads we heard gently
    butting the boards

that traversed the pit far below, made us afraid. We
    feared the swarm.
It was our thoughts though,
not Council steam, went down beneath the floor of
    the towering room

and the water lilies of the Chinese rug floated in light
into the furnace of stumbling wasps
to sense something that might make us welcome at a
    later date

burning out a gulf through the cracks and knot-holes,
      beneath the lid.
At times, it seemed innocuous,
a glue pot, a piecrust slapped on pocked timbers, a
      pat of swallow mud,

but at others, forgive me, we grew uncertain if the
      nest was glued to the house
or the house was glued to the nest.
At such times, it seemed the house was perched above
      a precipice

as if all its roots and foundations were suddenly flying
      out over it,
just hanging there, while
the wind of twenty thousand wings beneath it took
      its whole weight.

It was a summer of drought, and I stepped into the
      rug's radiance where
the great bay printed its shape
and I sensed the nest massage the soles of my bare
      feet like a jacuzzi of fire

and we wondered if perhaps it was a symbol of wealth
      sent to us,
or of bankruptcy, or both? There below
was it the windfall, or the bailiff's notice slapped on
      the dusty window?

Or was it a gateway? Again and again we dreamed
      the multitudes
of wasps, each one
among the many like a fizz in a helmet or an
      armourplated ohm

crumbling the breach, until the din filled our heads,
      rose above tape-hiss
and kettle, Mozart and the mains.
And we traced the vaguer image of ourselves in
      earphones

in the lens of the television once we had switched it
      off, seated as if
at one with the room's
curvaceous perspectives, in caps, unable to drown out
      the hum.

Was it some sort of centre, beneath our feet? It seemed
      to coincide
exactly with the balancing stem
of the rug's huge floppy lily. It seemed almost as if the
      stem led

further down into the heart of things, as if such solace
      depended
on such combustion,
perhaps, or as if somehow such depths of turbulence
      were required

to hold the petals so, stock still. The pit of crawling
      coals,
we dreamed, seemed to draw in
everything to itself like a cistern that fills and fills
      and fills

and melts the wax walls of its sides like smelting
      gold and dissolves
our shape and overflows
though the Chinese lily does not for a moment
      tremble. Nor change its pose.

A Dawn Composed in Various Shades of Green

We sleep on the last thought, wake to the first.
The train approaches us and things begin to shake.
Until you leave, we have to come back every morning
to this thick wanting, to every tiniest hair
standing erect, to the bruised familiar ghost
of our mouths, hovering and circling one another
in close orbit – though miles apart – as if you are
perpetually hanging over me, spilling all
the beautiful incoherent nonsense of want
like pidgin English, your fine, incessant rain.
To wake to find your eyes already open,
shoes on, your coat round your shoulders
or the weight of it off them, already slipping.
The bird in the belly is crashing and flapping.

Lines for Florentine Shadows

So much for the eyes of the chic Surrealist.
The fever in my brain – the mix of head-cold and sluicing about
of analgesics – puts this tilt on seeing:
the shadows of the table-legs, elongated three times
the length of their parabolas in the first café
to open up in the Piazza, mirror my vocal chords, *stretched*.
They are dainty as the spider on the cruet,
sieving some glorious matter or other
to this live show – an eclipse of brilliant particles.
When the ladder's loony tangent is skewing off west
and the bronze snout exceeding its own reach
and spun silver smelted by the bicycle's spokes
these bloom, from the circular table, like freakish petals
or a daylily of acrobats on stilts all day
choreographed in the ring around the ringmaster's
procession of *espressos* and altering squint.

Stendhal's Parrot

Unwell in Florence, dogged by the flu, dizzy on a diet
of frescoes and paracetamol, four parts ill
six overdosing on exquisiteness, I take the long way to the light.
At first there is the sense one hand
is airbrushed away, then half an ear, a toe, an index finger;
then half a torso, eroded by light.

I am stalked by Stendhal's similarly wilting ghost.
In the streets' gloomy canyons, streaked with sun, my mind's
like the seven leashes and seven Chihuahuas
in the old woman's one arthritic fist – smell out
the candlestreaked masterpiece, say, or climb
for the view, stop, eat *crostini*, just sit, stop, or hunker, panting.

The heavenly cycle lies in wait across the city
but my larynx is a swung bulb gagging on its thread
and every monument to human strength on the way
immune to sly viruses, not given to moods;
after the four hundredth stone step I tend
towards pure liquid, my knees dissolving, my mouth erased.

The great images grow stronger and more vivid the paler
and paler I wane, as if perilously see-through,
pale as the ether or the figure not-yet-painted,
the figure fading from the stucco. I step out of the gloom
into the molten brilliance, chewed to rags
by the light, glare white, and disappear.

The Evolution of Olives

Outside Florence's walls in the hissing grass
the olive-pickers snooze, under the olives;

one's hands lie across his chest, like the tomb-sleeper's;
his dusty boot thrown over the other's.

The ground around them, and the unattended fruit,
drink heat. Either the pickers are waiting

for their nets to sprout in the sun or for the olives
to invent a means of ripening slower.

Selling Parnassus

When a man sprays himself in white paint from head to foot
you can be sure he's selling something. His outfit
so *white*, his face, his gloves and hat, you might
imagine he'd been dipped in lacquer where he spins a plate
or spins a plate or two or spins the unspinnable plate
among Florence's monstrous sculptures. My shout
is weighty, he seems to say, my little body slight;
and you the crowd who must decide if what
I am is man, or sculpture. See how I shine from head to foot,
how I freeze, turn into marble, then speak out;
how I pose, unfreeze to speak, freeze to the spot.
Art must solicit attention, he mimes, with a slight
stoop, rather than wait for its public to come to it:
the stuff you queue for hours to see is on the life-support
machine, daubed for life under lamps, while art
should be effortlessly alive, and fluent, not
locked in some eternal gesture, trying to get out.
So he must speak and freeze, freeze and speak, and set
in the mould of his plaster-of-paris skin and outfit that
the Florentine boys can only barrack and berate,
as if their words might wash him clean of white
and bring his colour back, and make him more like them, or get
to form out of their soft demotic wit
a freak cloud just above his head about to spot and spit.

The Footwork of the Jazz Pianist

Odd that from this angle all we get to see
are shoes, socks (plus what never chose either) feet.
We get a glimpse of the ear of the artist
where the gleams of perspective offer it
while the feet dance, like street dolls, pumping thunder
through every striving knuckle of the beast
which shows us (who look across from under-
neath the level of the stage)
its butterfly belly, fat calves, its pig trotter castors.

Shoes, socks, feet, it is the footwork that tries
to persuade the dead weight of beast to go
to the lush grass at the limits of its chain and stake
for ever more delicate exercise.
And thunder moves over, doubles back, plunges in
the cavity of the belly and is borne
down through the stage-boards, as if to show
what dainty movements the neat feet make
when the head's in the storm.

Natsumi Surveys the Wide Wide River

1

The word is recently slapped upon the heel,
held upside down, a clamp on its navel.
The label on its ankle is in Japanese.

My language has one word to express
many ideas, requiring three in yours – this
English word is one third of a word.

The word is *curve* – because it is the first time
I have spoken it, nothing can cling;
it is pink and wrinkled, and carries with it

no trunk on castors (I think they're called).
You can see through it easily as you can
the foetus's skin stretched tight over the nut

of the brain, to view the simple workings:
it is word pure, brand new, with just
a little water of the birth bed dripping. Oh

curve – I run my finger along its edge, no dust;
it *bends*, like the universe,
like the morning road, unused

as the cuticle of a second-old fingernail,
or the skill light has to bend in the cold
and shock me strongly like the moon.

2

Another word is born! It contains
the magic particle that is the excited mood
of one more sleepy – they mate,

I try to say, they share one note that shivers.
The word is *resonance*. I hold it close.
And deep within the muffled walls

of a foreign language, its shiver must be strong.
I live in such a chamber, I know,
and for the note that murmurs on

and starts to die there is a smaller chance
of resonance (effect the same as word.)
My swift pupils, looking up at my tutor's,

wait for the sound to work – so this is
the trunk-call between me and the word,
and the note it strikes sets off the pause that hangs

between us, stretching out across
the South China Sea and Sea of Japan as far
inland as Kumamoto, where it arrives perhaps

seconds late, and waits during the delay
for reply to its little trust of hoping
a few pins tremble in their Oriental pot.

3
Observe how I am no longer yours
when speaking in my language, how I become
the youngest daughter of nine in love

with family and memory, who wishes to sing
of the sawdust lodged in grandpa's overalls
and of Junpei collecting cicada shells

or the creeper of fern-like leaves, purple flowers,
resting a wrist on the table. Note how I am
such fresh flowing water and follow

the current of feeling – compare me breathing
the oxygen of Japanese through every pore
and every strand thickly as garlic, with this

clogged sieve of translation to drip-feed
into your cloudy depths that do not clear
for a long while, once stirred up. I think

your many writers writing in your English wail
beneath the weight of the ink-well, past
and talking of the self, but I make

the wide crossing and dare to write
in your language as if just born
with words washed and wrinkled, longing for life.

In Praise of the Tenor Sax

She made it to the festival and went off with the saxophonist.
Not for love, he was not the likeliest object;
not for looks, which in truth were rather ordinary.
It was not for his height or stature, which were about average,
or nothing her friends would choose to comment on;
not for the pencil-line moustache that hovered
on his lip like light, as if uncertain of its provenance.
It was not for his quietness or his sudden blushes
or the air he gave off, say, of a diffident clerk
or the middle way he kept between wallflower and roué
or the limited language he had with which to speak
but for the fact that once he got behind his horn
he blew out such a lifelike energy he turned into the fender
and funnel and valves of the 00:00 express
which laid down its own track in darkness and flashed
through station after station as if choosing to ignore
the signal cocked at danger and compulsion to ease off
the throttle at its limit, but which stopped for her.

"This Island Seem to be Desert"

1
Your map was good and accurate, but
the longitude and latitude vague and so it was
difficult to find the centre, so far inland
of its own foaming reefs, the certainty of sea all round.
At it, the great churchly shadow stooped
over your cradle, washed by faith which shaped
the coastline as it did, cove and inlet, and grotto, and coral.
God was patient, at home, your love-object
and master of that weight of stone,
you knew, which would stop you flapping about:
the stones so very heavy, the light so named
and vegetation so unfragrant you knew that it would take
more than a minor shipwreck to bring in
the world in crates of lurid literature and white gin.

2
Now the track is laid way out over the gull-printed mud,
sleeper by sleeper, bolt by bolt, in your sleep:
down the glinting track you can smell the savour
of the guarded apples: *go, go, take this shape*
now your love-object takes the shape of someone else,
even this flawed, this all-too-human shape you choose,
they say, which will never sustain you like His.
Things shake, the train approaches, but you are
stuck on this island, with its limited library
and dominant father from whom the apples
draw all your attention to the vanishing point:
strain to see, *smell* them, way down the line they grow
to the size of obsession, as if to say
...there are only miles and miles of sea in your way.

Whisky Drinker Considers his Skirmish with Death

With so much hard ground rising to meet me I should be glad
    of a little sea.
What is heavier? Body or earth?
When they smack into each other they are of equal weight.
We do each other damage.

        The mangled cockpit, the churned up bank.

The windscreen spattered, as if muck snowed. This much I recall.
I was upside down
in the ditch, and a sky
of tussocks and puddles and hooves thundering upside down
tilted at my chin
and Wagner still boomed at the speakers, a wheel ticked
    to a standstill.

...*running water*, I thought, that is the sound of running water.

This much I recall – but what of the moment of rolling,
like being inside the drum of a washing machine,
those seconds, those milliseconds which I cannot ever re-enter,
when something *gasped* in mid air somewhat as if
it was the first leap
into the midwife's impersonal gloves, the drop over the edge:

all I *know* is, as I rolled, a rain of loose change fell to the ceiling
and my leaflets flapped and fluttered around me
like panicking birds trying to get the right way up.

        A soft regurgitation of Glenmorangie.
Then light, the bright light, of heaven?

        The policeman's lamp in the lane.
           I heard his umbrella unwrap, like wings.

Not yet, Mr Death, am I your punctured minion
    or your blue-eyed boy.

Charms against the Adultery

Things shake. These cloves and spells and these judgmental
       tongues
incline me even more to the liturgy of you,
your side of mouth, nape, your perineum;
to your remoter parts – your *Galapagos* – each one
a puddle containing the moon, each one
the greyhound's footprints laid down in the dew,
one at a time; and beyond this, well, to our species
of votive praise, we who crawl
through each other's armpits to create
the beast of four or fifty flailing arms,
four feet, two heads; who shed our surplus weight
like disapproval, or learn to use it as well
as we do this lack of good publicity which is
our rainforest ginseng, rhino pistle, our ambergris.

Alighieri's Lift

So Dante after all was not buried in Florence,
the smallprint informs us, but Ravenna:
bad enough to think of the body empty of the man
but now the tomb empty of the body;
better to have been surprised in Ravenna
than enlightened in Florence, I thought.
We opted to visit the empty tomb nonetheless;
while we waited on the hotel landing for the lift
(...the old cantankerous lift and cable that would feed us
down a shaft of god-knows-how-many feet)

a ponytailed man swept the cage up full of brilliant
                                            flowers,
primroses, gypsophila, arum-lilies
                spraying everywhere, as if to announce

the stone had been rolled away.

The Floodwaters

for Ted Hughes, 28 October, 1998

1

All day the floodwaters rose, like exequies,
they were dragging up the muck and roaring yellow;
they carried off the praying stool, lectern and armchair.
I heard like a panic of bird-flight the racket
of the hailstones in the conservatory:
there was a sense of orphaned mischief in the sound,
of the sudden, open, blowing view;
one at a time the breakable hundred panes.

We lament our lost fathers, who leave the view clear,
who grow ever more untalkative though wise.
And here was a sound, of unfathered hail
and poetry's canvas flapping on its ropes, flapping;
water rose from below... the Severn
up twenty foot, the Wye fifteen, with news
of sixty rivers on red flood alert, freak hailstones
the size of marbles, record rainfall and gales.

All day they rose and bulged, the waters of chaos,
trapping the ironmonger in the room upstairs,
the tiny boy rowing through the traffic-lights.
This was the day you died, when sandbags were piled high
and the floodwaters flexed and spread into ocean
as if confused, as if trying though blind
to find a level or pour like the displacement
of water after *The Pequod* into the hole.

2

Between the sinking and the yellow swell,
so white against the water ebbing in
the swan is swimming through the Swan Hotel.

The great river, scorning sandbag and sill,
broke window glass and poured on in.
Between the sinking and the yellow swell,

between the elusive and palpable,
against the cloudy Severn bulging in
the swan is swimming through the Swan Hotel.

It cuts the path lanky waiters will,
down the siding of rooms left floating in
between the sinking and the yellow swell.

Between the white, the very white and optical,
like pale gas against leaf-viridian
the swan is – swimming through the Swan Hotel

where the plunder lodges but cannot keep still,
against the current, against the weir's din,
between the sinking and the yellow swell
the swan is swimming through the Swan Hotel.

3

And how will the decks balance, how will the ark
stand up, without its drogue stone? Without
the brake that eases it through the depths,
holds it upright, parting the brilliant shoals?

How will the ark be steadied without the stone,
slow down, or pause? How will it be held
now the long spine is withdrawn although
the notches crave their mortices, nerves fly about?

How will it accommodate the tidal bulges
of the yellow century, distinguish between
the shoals and the swell of it pushing up
the topography of the new washed world?

How will it fare in the way ahead, trawling light,
without the bowed and lengthy beam
cut from a single tree? The drogue stone is off,
I swear, and the hull of the ark begins to spin.

Circle Line

Something is about to happen. The Underground wind
must first withdraw before it can come in again.
Sucked back, it snatches the scraps on the tide
and dances them, pours up our sleeves

and inside our buttons, finds skin, and sends
an elaborate shudder down our spines.
You stand beside me, impassive and composed,
in your long black coat and cloche hat,

flashing glances beneath your fringe:
rails produce a fizz – a clicking connection – as if
we can actually see the electricity
which conducts past to future, the papers to the wind,

power to the filament, the static to your hair,
your gloved hand to my colder, naked hand.
Something is about to happen. It always is.
The papers blow, crowd shifts, the high steel starts to shiver,

and the lid is off the unbroken circuit
which connects me to you, one event to the next;
it is fierce as the seeds of a fizzing hailstorm
but one that never falters, never sleeps.

The piles of mint-condition copies and the gleam-flotilla
of glasses, yet to be filled, are streets off:
the charges are spitting between us and them,
from rails into our ankles, our ankles into the rails.

And you lean towards me, holding on, and the wind gets up
and the papers dance and we take a step
towards the platform-edge, and way down the line a light
clicks over soundlessly from stop, to go.

Death of a Whippet

Or perhaps I see it less as whippet
than ribs in a coil of energy, a flame in a cage
that steps out across the asphalt as if
flowing in all directions at once.

See how it walks on its feet, goes up
and down, down and up like a seasick sail
pegged to the hump of its spine
or a current, wearing its molars upfront, in a smile.

When it bounces off the bumper
onto the bonnet and onto the windscreen
like a botched spring, a pelt
tucked nose to tail it simply unravels

and lopes away and breaks into a run
up into reefs of cloud and away over trees
and finally out of sight, hair up, too terrified:
and now there is no dog for us to see,

just the appalling notion of its demise
and stench of diesel, no mess, no broken bone:
asphalt and altocumulus survive
the meeting of whippet and truck in the lane.

Tai Kwando Lessons for the Men in Cloth

Yes and Wittgenstein for footballers,
Sartre for lifeboatmen, sou'westers for the bookish,

bromide for high hurdlers and Uzis for the meek.
Under siege our pastors, leaving their bicycles outside,

give us the breaking news on evolution.
One has a pistol in the grandfather clock,

another an alarm, poised like an urban pulse,
beneath the treadle. One dreams the barricades

of inert pews stacked up in a hurry
and wakes in a sweat. Now the once administered-to

are administering threats our men in cloth must develop
unaccustomed moves, inducting us towards

the new nature which is so sublimely contrary.
In the scummed heat-trap of the canal, the fish

leap up through gnat-storms to blunt the hook.
Now the mouse retreats, the Gorgonzola advances.

Once it was the parish under threat from the church.
Whatever glimpse you steal of our congenial ministers

filleted so precisely, as if by blinds,
through the gymnasium's monkey-bars, those heads

so high up in the clouds have no idea whatever
their mint condition trainers kick so hard at far below.

The Deaf School

Not the Institute, but the place the deaf girl took me to,
obeying as it did
roughly the same laws of perspective:

bare of indulgence, of sound, of bloom,
the end of the line
for the scaffolder's blunder, horn, the playground's scream.

Bare walls – an odd foreshortening–
and a sense
of hieroglyphics hidden, so to speak, in moving currents

like the light that lapped and flowed from end to end
as the blind knocked,
as the pencil rolled, without soundtrack.

Strange all my attempts to reach the deaf woman should
imply she had
something I did not. Sat opposite her, I'll not deny

I saw myself reflected, as if wholly visible,
deprived
by her deafness of language, unable to speak.

I was disturbed by her focus – by those rapid pupils
brought
to finger-exercises, sans violin, sans bow:

and I sensed her absorb through the voiceless boom,
through her soles, her calves,
up through her pelvic arch, by degrees my indefinite noise.

Though our patient interpreter broke brilliant crumbs
between us, I knew
in the blind's gusts of light pale Karen was both

prospect of water and of sighted island,
and I
the churning ferry, its clapperless bell.

Leaving Auxi

The swallows crazier and crazier in the yard
as if to say goodbye. First, the children,
then their Wellingtons, stranded in the mud.
There was the checking under the bed again,
the backward glance into the tidied kitchen;
the ghosts of our quarrels haunting the *gite*
like the stormflies the bulb, overwhelmed by daylight;
and the tape caught between the bumper and the thorn
unravelling on its racy spools behind
for the length of the whole drive. Madame shouted
after us, anchoring the place in the mirror:
...quelqu'un ne jouera jamais plus de Mozart.
The trees slid over the windscreen and sunlight flashed us
through convex glass, where we sat a little apart
in our changed composure, in sunglasses that
set the early world and each other in a brown cast,
like sepia. I thought of the continuous
signal of joy exposed like a film in the dirt.
You slipped another tape into the deck,
enquired: *do we really have to put up with this Bach?*

The Bunker

The Monchy children posing for the school photographer
knew nothing of its whereabouts, nor would they think
of such a thing buried somewhere

in the brambles of their amiable neighbourhood,
the monstrous, immovable anchor supporting so
fragile a structure of convolvulus as if it bore

the petals of the gas upon it, lit into flames.
Only a book, long out of print, ringed a location,
only this neurological map divining a route.

I thrashed through the corn, that lashed and ripped
at my bare knees while my trainers – so *white* –
absorbed the mud at the roots like lights going out.

I imagined it ahead of me, the boiling casement
of six foot thick concrete stuffed with darkness:
a hundred tons of fluid and stones set hard

around the slit through which the soul crouched
inside its second casement, a spirit bubble –
it was a dried up source, I thought, the Kaiser's tentacle,

or a root buried too deep to ever dig out,
spreading deeper and deeper while elephantine brambles
broke across the surface, with eight foot nettles:

I waded in through, stung from ankle to cheek,
and felt for a moment the hairs stand up on my neck:
Get out of here, leave it. What lies here belongs

to the dried blood and flies. A way back, the photographer is
cajoling softly and the group of bright faces,
empty of anything, stares through him into future.

In Italy (by Match-light)

"And I saw what looked like an angel, holding
in his hand the key to the Abyss..."
Revelation 20:1

Once more he'll get the blob of sulphur to burst
alight, cupped so it will burn up:
see what you can, while you can. See, in

the sudden match's yellow-blue explosion,
your father's features: intent pupils,
nose-bridge, khaki collar and, in each pupil, *flame.*

Because the – *fucking* – kerosene lamp withholds
its merry wick he must read
by the light of matches your mother's insect-scrawl:

see the army tent's sail full of sulphur
sailing him, sailing him
ever further south – flapping and drumming.

On the crease of his brow a mosquito,
a moth's gigantic shadow purring across the page.
And this the last match. Be assured

he'll burn thumb and forefinger, pinched nails,
before he lets the last go out,
so bright. See how the charred stalk dips

against the entrusted dark, the match-wood hissing
to nose fluid forward, yielding to flame.
A while longer light. A while longer.

Every thought of him – like the orange nimbus
itself, or warplans he serves without understanding –
drawn to the sulphur's tear

                    like insects off the river.

Lovesongs in the Digital Age

With all that comes to you as first born comes the gift
of flight – through grid after grid of the satellite map
your heart's dispersal perfectly shadows
the weather's creeping influence cast out

over the world – red, into green, into gold; its shape
changes from second to second,
and will again, and will again: to email ports
in St Petersburg, Erinsborough, Calgary – at sixteen –

you export your likeness in baseball cap and by return
your teenage girls kick in, as if just born:
under the pressure building in their clothing
their mouths are also changing shape, who live at ease

in this flying mental realm but balk at flesh.
Who meet you, through thousands of miles flashed
to the finest division of light which is to transcend
geography, Alp and cupola, and plant in your head

the seed, your Huguenot name blooming in theirs:
Leerdit? Lyardee? L'Idiot? Liararat?
The coastline of the great hormonal storm
creeping from grid to grid seems set to trace how love
throws an awning of pixels over the globe.

Flight of Twins

Your twin, mother, the shedding of your twin
ensured your ascent. If one had to sink away, the other
had to rise, for two, you were left with the knowledge
of a profound intimacy breathing there
over your left shoulder, always to the left,

always there taking your lead, a grey sleepy eye.
At eighty, still you dream you pass through her in
the rotating doors of the white hotel in Venice
or descending the Metro steps, into warm wind, trying
            to place her.
You dream of her toothache, her levy of dentists;

the twelfth breakage in a year of her left wrist;
her monopoly of the common cold.
She was always just a little to the left of you
and still is, dreaming you are to the right.
At first, the lack of space pushed you over to one side

so that one arm – at times mistaken for hers –
grew stronger than the other, and your feet
once sole-to-sole with hers – began to climb over,
ascending as if softly the ladder of her.
Your arms and your mouth were hungrier and drew in

all that you needed; she sunk away
into the water, without a name, like a skein of weed
with bubbles in its mouth – and you so full of calcium, as if
            the light
you pushed for through the pelvic arch was a lock
and you the fresh-cut, formidable key.

To the God of Rain

i.m. Gregor Fisk (1973-1997)
who suffered from Cerebral Palsy

A dry tap, Father, I was a dry tap
Expecting the news of water –

At birth, the savage coulters
Of my mother's pelvis drawn

Through my brain's clay left it
Rutted and squeezed out of shape,

Lord, baffled like raw soil;
Nothing grew in it, and you

Knew better than I what would
Be my salvaged crop.

There was this bit of scrap,
The sliced sod. This glossy furrow.

There was this space. Forgive me,
I'd always thought you'd teach me,

Lord, how to be wise,
But my thoughts were like moths

Thumping in the webs;
There was this space on my brow.

How could this shapeless big body,
This slowness to follow

And inner wilderness in need
Of water be squeezed

Through the narrow eye,
Lord, of the citadel's needle?

There was this space. This space.
There was this space on my brow

Which awaited the licks of your rain.

Re-reading *Lolita* in a Tropical Climate

I count them, one by one, the tropical insects which
negotiate their almost weightless mass
down the underslope of page sixty-seven,
seventy-one and seventy-two (fluttering) or out along
the high guillotined edge first of page ninety-eight
then of ninety-nine (collapsing) as if
drawn to the savour blowing there
in a breeze of suggestion, while the heat drains
every ray it can out of the Times New Roman
and softly buckles the wove and bakes it hotter and hotter
until it is a shimmering, alabaster mirage
inviting you to wade it; note how
the cover also bends in a slow curve
as the undertow withdraws, bent back
like the curl of a wave, gathering as if to break.
Wasp, three times the size of the English variety,
green-helmeted fly rubbing its hands in the sun,
mosquito – so frail to drink in avarice – or
the locked couple coupling, one by one, are drawn
by the scent and the taste and the hunger
on this their daylight odyssey from flails of sugar
to this plantation of ur-vowels – from
the trickle in the clavicle to the lovers'
wet gluteal cleft, to the rotting peach,
the gashed market melon to the sex-smell
of Nabokov in minus time, feet still sticky, helmet bright.
Tempting to picture a man sat reading
at the circular white table, sweating and bitten
in the outer physical world of heat
while language builds him an equally boiling one
image by image – I wave away the insects.
They both descend and rise, one by one,
whose legs if magnified ten times would visibly

bend the surface of the typeface
they do not quite puncture – as if such feet
distort the membrane between worlds.
As huge capricious clouds
pour over at speed, I read
of huge capricious clouds. One dream.
The membrane is taut as cellophane.
The plump fly thumps on both sides of it at once.

For the Acquisition of Reading Spectacles

Language returns, lewd and vivid, to the page.
It is a catwalk of cheek-bones and pushy femmes,

of voile, of silk, perfectly focused. I ogle
its slinky points and hips and crevices.

If once my eyesight drove it from the stage
it comes back, strutting its trash-chic, to steal

the photo shoot and set its models swivelling
on their suspiciously high heels.

The light starts flickering, to subtitles.
A universe hides behind a blade of grass, we know,

so how much more of it will hide
out of sight in the wings – roady,

baggage-boy and impressario – behind the hips
of these svelte or bullish creatures?

Monsieur le Verb in slatted leather, avec le bulge,
le butterfly-tattoo, le civilised snarl.

La Grandame Adjective in les gossiping mauves,
in drag, organza camisole, that tulle.

Les cross-dressers, in le skimpy lycra, swopping
dusky pink for crimson, crimson for dusky pink;

Mademoiselle la Metaphor to oohs and ahs
in seethrough chemise and, beneath it, skin.

Rain

There is the line from Verlaine I will not recall....
Borges

I went to sleep striking agreements with death
and woke inspecting every blade of grass:
green, the word, I spoke it for the first time.
Light, the taste, I smelt it for the first time.
Rain like light, intensifying green.
My skin grew babylike, so long immersed,
my pupils balanced in their proper space.
Light on grass, I tasted it for the first time.
Rain on grass, on green, intensifying both.
Rain like green, made visible by light.
I was miracle engineering, honed to tips.
And I knew you were green, were light, were grass,
you were the provenance of rain.
Green, the self, became each other.
Rain, the word, the rite of growth.
If this was love, then what was not?
When there is no other word the word is love.

Acknowledgements

Acknowledgements are due to the editors of the following magazines and newspapers in which some of these poems first appeared, or will appear: *Ambit, The Independent, Leviathan Quarterly, London Magazine, New Writing 8, New Writing 10, New Writing 11, Poetry London Newsletter, Poetry Review, Poetry Wales, The Rialto, Stand, Thumbscrew.*

'Distiller's Unstable Daughter Explains her Absence from the Class' (coupled with 'Santa Pelted with Eggs' – not included in this collection) first appeared in *New Writing 8*, edited Norfolk and Fischer, Vintage/The British Council, 1999. 'The Wasps' Nest' first appeared in *New Writing 10*, edited Szirtes and Lively, Picador/The British Council, 2001. 'In Praise of the Tenor Sax' first appeared in *New Writing 11*, edited O'Hagan and Tóibín, Picador/The British Council, 2002. 'Paris' and 'The Floodwaters' first appeared in *Poetry Wales* and *Thumbscrew*, respectively, and have subsequently been revisited. 'Stendhal's Parrot', 'The Evolution of Olives', 'A Dawn Composed in Various Shades of Green', 'Circle Line' and 'Alighieri's Lift' were first broadcast on BBC radio.

I am extremely grateful for the Hawthornden Fellowship in April-May 2002 which enabled me to finish this book, in expansive space; and to my employers at Bath Spa University College – particularly Tim Middleton and Richard Kerridge – for supporting me during this period. Thanks also to The Royal Literary Fund without whose outright grants the book would have taken a great deal longer to appear, and to Fiona Clark and Eileen Gunn, in particular, for their support. Personal thanks to Michael Hulse for endorsing the title poem at a time when the book was losing its way; to Vuyelwa Carlin for her judicious insight and to Fiona Sampson for her bravura reading of the manuscript; to Don Paterson for restoring my faith in the whole project. And to Miranda Liardet for her beautiful endurance.

By the same author:

Clay Hill
Fellini Beach
Competing with the Piano Tuner